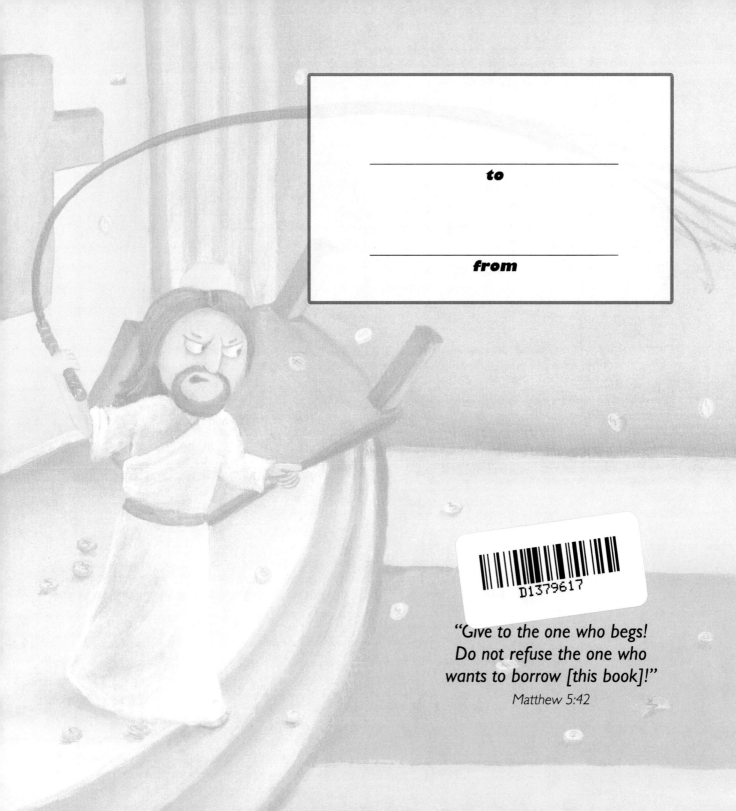

_____
to

_____
from

"Give to the one who begs!
Do not refuse the one who
wants to borrow [this book]!"
Matthew 5:42

AWKWARD BIBLE

Awkward Moments (Not Found In Your Average) Children's Bible - Volume #2
Copyright ©2014 Awkward Bible
Text Copyright ©2014 Awkward Bible
Illustration Copyright ©2014 Awkward Bible

Awkward Moments (Not Found In Your Average) Children's Bible - Volume #2
©2014 Awkward Moments. All Rights Reserved. First Printing: 2014.
ISBN-13: 978-0692264980
ISBN-10: 0692264981
BISAC: Humor / Topic / Religion
See all of our books at: www.AwkwardMomentsBible.com
Requests for any additional information should be addressed to info@awkwardmomentsbible.com

The editorial arrangement, analysis, and professional commentary are subject to this copyright notice. No portion of this book may be copied, retransmitted, reposted, duplicated, or otherwise used without the express written approval of the author, except by reviewers who may quote brief excerpts in connection with a review.

Any unauthorized copying, reproduction, translation, or distribution of any part of this material without permission by the author is prohibited and against the law.

All scripture verses contained within are taken from the The Holy Bible - Yet Another Man's Version (YAMV) - a fictitious and paraphrased work developed for the purpose of this book from public domain sources. Any similarity to a previously copyrighted work is pure coincidence and understandable as the quoted scriptures are paraphrased from the same various sources of ancient texts in the the public domain from which all Bible translations are based. No permission from any Bible publishers is implied (nor needed). All rights reserved.

Disclaimer and Terms of Use: This book is a comedic parody. No information contained in this book should be considered as scholarly sourced or cited material. Your reliance upon information and content obtained by you at or through this publication is solely at your own risk. Awkward Moments or the authors assume no liability or responsibility for damage or injury to you, other persons, or property arising from any use of any product, information, idea, or instruction contained in the content or services provided to you through this book. Reliance upon information contained in this material is solely at the reader's own risk.

Written By: Horus Gilgamesh, horus@awkwardmomentsbible.com
Illustrated By: Agnes Tickheathen, agnes@awkwardmomentsbible.com

Media Inquiries: info@awkwardmomentsbible.com

Awkward Moments

Not Found In Your Average

Children's Bible

Volume #2

Written by **Horus Gilgamesh**
Illustrated by **Agnes Tickheathen**

"I love the tension this book brings..."

As a Christian, I love the Bible and believe it is 100% inspired by God and trustworthy. I am also a big fan of the entire *Awkward Moments (Not Found In Your Average) Children's Bible* series of books and online articles. Given my role as an evangelical pastor and seminary professor, that may sound like quite a contradictory statement. However, I have held up my well-read copy of Vol. #1 from the pulpit on many occasions and used it as an example and learning tool in church as I teach. Now, please let me explain why...

Over the last two years, Horus and I have formed what may seem like an unlikely friendship - a devout Christian leader and an "apostate" author who often challenges the very core of my beliefs. However, coming from similar pasts, we have come to learn that we have friends and mentors in common, even hobbies and tastes in movies and music in common. More importantly, we have a common interest in Biblical literacy - getting people to actually open their Bibles and think critically about the words on the page and their impact in their lives, and on society. As Horus pointed out in the first book, while the Bible might be the bestselling book of all time, according to a recent Pew Research study, more than half of practicing Christians couldn't name the four Gospels - the first four books of the New Testament. Regardless of our divergent views of faith, Horus is absolutely right - Christians have a Biblical literacy problem.

For far too long, many Christians haven't thought too much about what they read in the Bible. Or worse (in my opinion) - they might not even read the Bible at all. Perhaps they mainly re-read the pleasant verses that bring them comfort or reflect on certain stories they first learned as young children back in Sunday school or from a sermon. Yet, they often don't go any deeper - never opening their own Bibles and reading the whole thing, or investigating a pastor's sermon - maybe never thinking about it again from an adult's perspective later in life. As a result, when a book like this pulls certain stories or verses out to the forefront, it can be quite "awkward." Understandable reactions range from confusion to even anger that no one pointed out these verses before to them. What I appreciate about this book is that it forces Christians to examine the Bible – which is something we should have been doing all along!

What is very important to understand, however, is why I am writing this foreword to begin with. As a pastor, teacher and student of the Bible, I would assert that there are responses to every one of the Awkward Moments you will find in this book. These passages have not just recently been discovered by Horus - they have always been in the Bible, and scholars throughout history have spent their lives investigating the most "awkward" stories found in scripture. When you look at the historical setting of the Bible's origins - who wrote each of the books and the audience for whom they were originally written, it makes all the difference in how we come to understand scripture. What may even sound mythical or like a fairy tale becomes understood in the context of the original readers and each author's intent. When you do study them, you then see more clearly why these specific passages sound so awkward at first reading. For me and for many others throughout history, it does not cause loss of belief in the Bible at all. It actually caused me to trust it even more.

Another point to make is that when you read the awkward stories in the Bible, just because something that happened is written down in the Bible doesn't mean that God approved it. You may not have noticed certain stories in the Bible before, but what I love is that God did not remove the very awkward parts to only give us a nice sanitary Bible. In fact, it is quite the opposite - God wanted to show the grittiness and brokenness of humanity - including the good, the bad and the awkward.

This messy, ancient depiction of broken humanity is quite real and allows us to see ourselves living right in the middle of it - leading us to better understand why we need Jesus. As I mention Jesus, please make sure you are reading the full story of Jesus, not simply the awkward sounding parts of his story in isolation without full Biblical context.

One last thing to know as you read this, is that there have been many scholars of literature who knew the difference between mythical and literal literature. For example, C.S. Lewis and J.R.R. Tolkien were devout Christians who believed in the Bible. You have scientists like Francis Collins, founder of the Human Genome Project who believes in the Bible. You have musical artists like Johnny Cash and even Alice Cooper who are believers in the Bible. They know these awkward stories, and also know that there are responses to them when you take the time to fully study them properly. I could go on and on giving responses for each illustration in this book, but - I might just save that for a book of my own in the near future.

In the meantime, I hope you are challenged and stretched while reading this book - but don't let it stop there. Don't only engage in a surface view of the Bible by reading the verses shown in this book and then jumping to conclusions. I urge you to dig deeper and take the time to better understand the true complexity of each book of the Bible.

I love the tension this book brings, and I hope it causes many readers to become students of the Bible wanting to know more about the Jesus it reveals. Like Horus, my hope is that you will read the whole story - not just a couple verses here and there, passed on by your pastor, or even a book like this. If it takes a shockingly "awkward" illustration of Jesus depicted as a pyromaniac vine to open up John 15, so be it! At the end of the day, some of the Bible can sound quite awkward, indeed. But it is a life changing, amazing book. Please join me in opening up your favorite Bible and reading along with this challenging book - from Genesis to Revelation!

Dan Kimball
Vintage Faith Church in Santa Cruz, CA
Master of Arts, Western Seminary
Doctor of Ministry, George Fox University
www.facebook.com/dankimball

The First Lie

The Lord warned Adam, "You may eat from any tree in the garden except the tree that gives knowledge about good and evil. If you eat fruit from that tree, on that day you will certainly die!"

Genesis 2:16-17

The First Question

Hearing the sound of the Lord walking through the garden in the cool of the day, the *[only]* man *[on earth]* and his wife hid behind a tree. So, the *[all-knowing, all-powerful]* Lord called out for the man *[the only man on earth]*, **"Adam, where art thou?"**

Genesis 3:8-9

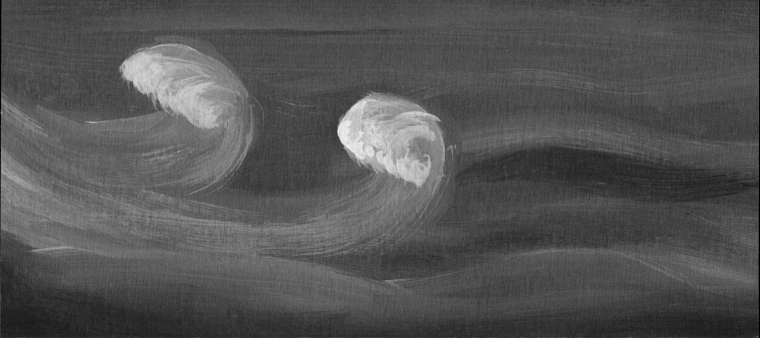

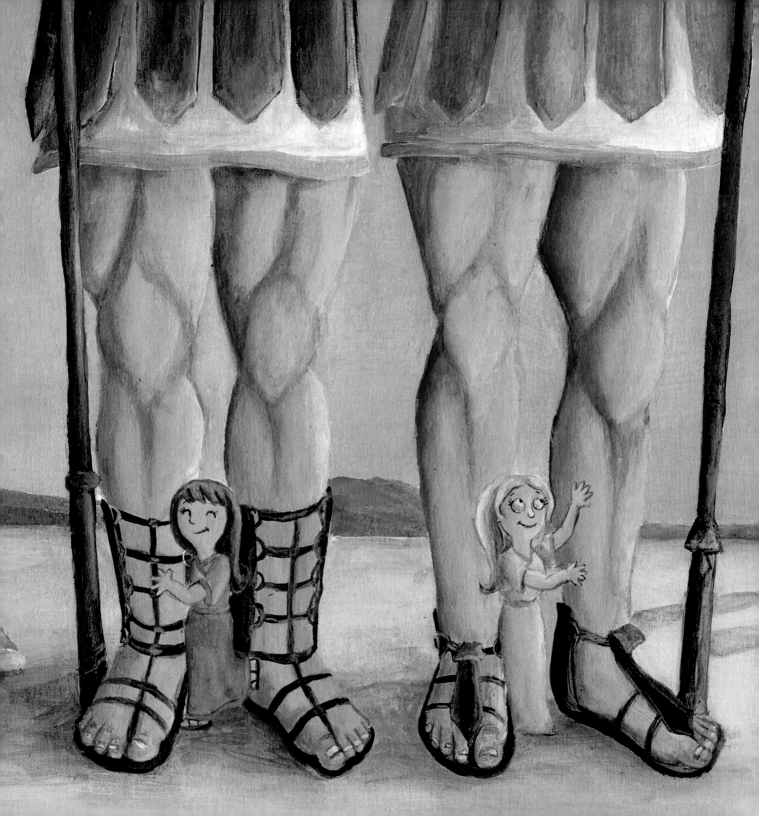

Giant Gigolos

When humans began to multiply across the earth, the Sons of God saw that the daughters of humans were very beautiful and took them as wives for themselves - whomever they chose. The Lord said, "People are only human and I won't let them bother my Spirit forever. I will only let them live for 120 years." Giant warriors known as the Nephilim were on the earth.

The Sons of God had sex with human women, giving birth to children who became heroes, famous warriors of ancient times.

Genesis 6:1-4

The spies brought back the bad news to Israel, "Those who go there will be destroyed! All of the people we saw were giants! We even saw the Nephilim there! Compared to them, we look like tiny grasshoppers in their sight!"

Numbers 13:32-33

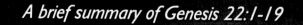

A brief summary of Genesis 22:1-19

Dangerous Obedience

Abraham hears God's voice telling him to kill his only son.
Without a single question, Abraham agrees to kill Isaac.
As a reward for his obedience, God blesses Abraham
and his family for many generations.

The End.

(The other details of this story hardly seem relevant.)

Like Any Proud Parent

All of the people of the earth used one language and were working together to build an amazing city with a tower that could reach up to heaven. They said, "This will make a name for us so we won't end up scattered across the earth!"

The Lord saw them talking together and working together and said, "This is only the beginning of what they can do. Soon they might be able to do anything they want!" So, the Lord stopped the city from being built. Then He confused the people's language and scattered them across the earth so they would no longer be able to understand each other or work together.

Genesis 11:1-8

My Own Grandpa

After God turned Lot's wife into a pillar of salt,
the man lived in a cave with his two daughters.
"Our dad is old," the older girl told her sister.
"Let's get him drunk with wine so we can take turns
having sex with him until we get pregnant to keep our
family's name alive!" So, for the next two nights they
got their dad drunk and took turns having sex with him.
Both of Lot's daughters became pregnant with his two
sons/grandsons, Moab and Ben-Ammi - the fathers of
the Moabite and Ammonite tribes.

Genesis 19:30-38

"In this corner, The Omni-...?"

A man appeared and wrestled with Jacob until just before dawn. When the Man saw that He could not win the match, He touched Jacob on the hip and dislocated the joint. They kept wrestling until the Man finally said, "Let go of me! It's almost daylight."

"You can't go until you bless me," Jacob replied. Then the Man asked, "What is your name?"- "Jacob," he answered, and the Man said, "Your name will no longer be Jacob. You have wrestled with God and with men, and you have won. That's why your name will be Israel." Jacob then demanded, "Tell me your name," and the Man asked, "Don't you know who I am?" He blessed Jacob, who said, "I have seen God face to face, and I am still alive." So Jacob named the place Peniel, meaning "Face of God."

Genesis 32:24-32

Moses Meets A Bush

Moses was worried that the Israelites wouldn't believe that God had appeared to him (as a bush). So, God (the bush) turned Moses' walking staff into a serpent and back into a staff as proof! Then God (the bush) turned Moses' hand leprous, as white as snow, then back to normal as proof. Last but not least, God (the bush) told Moses that he could turn water into blood by pouring it on the ground. "That will prove it!" said ... (the bush). *Exodus 4:1-9*

~~Pro-Life? Pro-Choice?~~ <u>No Choice!</u>

The Lord told Moses, "Tell the Israelites this: If a man suspects his wife has sinned and become impure by having sex with another man, he must take her to the priest! (With a grain offering.)

The priest will force the woman to stand before the Lord. He will take some dirt from the floor of the Holy Tent and add it to some special water in a clay jar. He will loosen her hair and force the woman to promise to tell the truth, 'If you have committed no sin, this potion will cause no harm. But, if you have sinned against your husband and drink this water - **your baby will die inside you!** You will never be able to have children ever again! And the Lord will curse you so that others will speak evil of you.'

The priest will wash these words off his scroll into the water and force the woman to drink the potion. Regardless of the outcome, the husband will not be guilty of anything. But, if the woman has sinned, she will suffer greatly and her unborn baby will die inside her.

This is the law."

Numbers 5:11-31
(summarized)

Talking Out Of His censored

The next day God became angry and sent his angel to stop Balaam. After Balaam hit his ass for the third time, the Lord caused Balaam's ass to speak, "Why are you angry at me? What have I ever done to deserve being hit three times?" Balaam told his ass, "You made me look like a fool! If I had a sword, I would kill you right here!" But his ass argued, "Look, I am your ass. You have sat on me for many years and you know that I have never done this before!"

Balaam agreed, "That is true." Then the Lord allowed Balaam to see His angel standing in the road, holding a sword, asking - "Why did you hit that ass three times? I am the one who came to stop you, but your ass saw me and turned away. If your ass had not protected you, I would have killed you already! But, I would have left your ass alone!"

Numbers 22:21-35

32 For The Lord

"Why have you let the women live? They followed Balaam's advice and caused the people of Israel to rebel against the Lord at Mount Peor. You must kill them all - every man, woman, and child, **_except_** the young virgin girls. Keep the virgins for yourselves." - Moses
(Except for the thirty-two virgins that the Lord demanded for Himself.)

Numbers 31:15-41

Why Can't I Quit You?

King Saul had a son named Jonathan and a servant named Jesse who had a son of his own, named David. When Jonathan and David first met, they were knit together at the soul. Because of their love for one another, they made a covenant. Jonathan removed his robe and gave it to David. He also gave his garments, even his sword, and his bow, and his girdle to the son of his family's servant.

King Saul became jealous of David's success and blessings from the Lord and wanted him dead, tricking Jonathan into bringing David to him. When Saul tried to kill David, he escaped to live with Samuel and was able to evade more attempts on his life.

David returned to ask Jonathan, "What have I done wrong? Why is your father trying to kill me?" Jonathan replied, "This can't be true! I can't believe it!" David explained, "Your father knows very well that you have come to look favorably on me. He'll kill me."

"I will do anything you want me to," said Jonathan. Then Jonathan made David reaffirm his vow of love again, for Jonathan loved David as he loved his own soul. David fled again.

When Saul found out, he was very angry with Jonathan, saying, "You son of a perverse, rebellious woman! Do you think I don't know that you have chosen the son of our own servant to your own shame, and to the shame of your mother's nakedness? Bring David to me - he is dead!" When Jonathan asked his father, "Why do you want to kill David? What did he do wrong?," the King threw his spear across the room and tried to kill his own son. Now knowing that his father desperately wanted to kill David, Jonathan became angry and left the table. He was so upset and angry with his father that he refused to eat any food. His father had humiliated him and wanted to kill David.

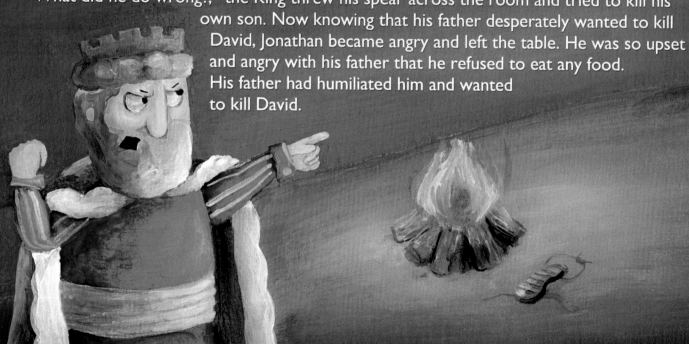

David came out of hiding and bowed three times before Jonathan. They kissed one another, and wept one with another, until David exceeded. It was a very sad goodbye, especially for David. Jonathan said, "Go in peace. We have taken a vow in the Lord's name that will bind us forever. You and me, your seed and my seed, together!" David rose and escaped Jonathan's father again.

When David later heard about Jonathan's death, he tore his clothes and cried - singing, "I weep for you, my brother Jonathan! Oh, how much I loved you! How wonderful was your love for me, far beyond the love from any woman!"

[The Lord continued to bless David's lineage in preparation of the coming Messiah...]

I Samuel 18 - 2 Samuel 1

Sending A Message

David told Nathan, "I have sinned against the Lord." Nathan replied, "The Lord will forgive you, even for this sin. But for showing contempt for the Lord, your new baby son will die."

The Lord struck the baby and caused him to become very sick. David begged God to spare the innocent child. He would not eat and lay on the bare ground all night. The elders of his family begged him to get up and eat with them, but he refused.

On the seventh day the baby had died. "How can we tell David?" the servants asked. "He wouldn't reason when the boy was sick. Now that he's dead, David might harm himself."

But, when David heard that his son was dead, he rose from the floor, washed and changed clothes. After going to worship the Lord, he asked his servants to make food to eat. Then he ate.

2 Samuel 12: 13-20

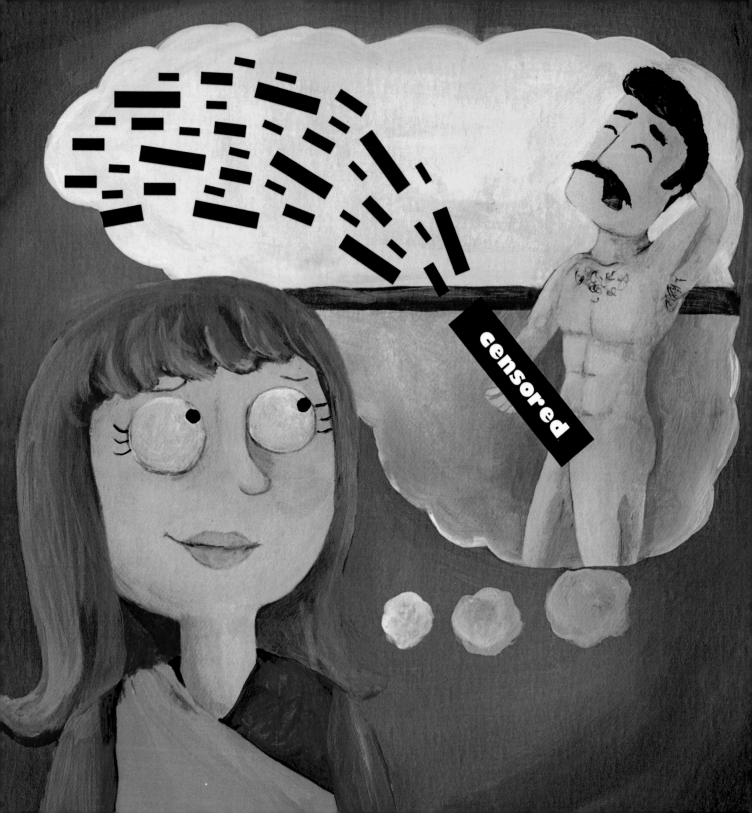

A Whore's Punishment

Oholibah lusted after lovers with genitals as large as a donkey's and their seminal emission was as strong as that of stallions. Remembering her youth, when Egyptians fondled her young nipples and squeezed her young breasts.

Therefore, the Lord says, "I will send your lovers against you from every direction - even those you rejected. They will surround you from every side. I will hand you over to them for punishment so they can do with you as they please. I will turn my jealous anger against you, and they will deal harshly with you. They will cut off your nose and ears. Your children will be taken and everything you own will be burned. They will strip you of your clothes and jewels - slaughtering by the sword!

They will treat you with hatred and rob you of all you own, leaving you stark naked. This is your fault and your shame will be exposed to all the world. I will force you to drink from your sister's cup of terror - filled to the brim with scorn and derision, distress and desolation. You will drink it all and smash the cup to pieces, plucking off your breasts in anguish. Yes, you will suffer the full penalty. Then you will know I am the Lord!"

Ezekiel 23:19-49

Reinstating The Draft

The Lord carried me away to a valley filled with dry bones and told me what to say, "Dry bones, listen to the word of the Lord! I am going to make you live again!"

Suddenly, there was a rattling noise across the valley. The bones came together, skeletons, muscles and flesh. Skin formed and breath came into their bodies. The dry bones came to life and stood up on their own feet, a great army!

Ezekiel 37:1-10

Potty Training

God told the priests, "If you don't listen to me and honor me, I will send a curse upon you and I will curse your blessings too! Actually, I have already cursed them because you don't take me seriously! I will punish your children, and I will spread dung on your faces, the dung from your animal sacrifices - and you will be thrown away like any other garbage. Then you will know that I am the Lord!"

Malachi 2:2-4

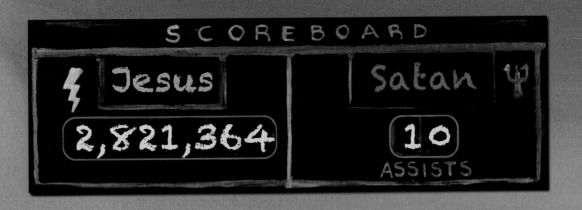

No Damsel, No Distress

"It's still missing something. A hero's conflict, maybe?"

"What if we added the old 'damsel in distress' bit? Audiences love that stuff. Then, we can bring in the authorities as bullies who are trying to trick the hero so they can frame him."

"Great idea! Yeah, and the hero plays it really cool, like James Dean. Aloof and mysterious."

"But, what happens to the bad guys?"

"It doesn't matter, they'll just disappear - the audience won't even notice, they'll only care about the sexy girl and the hero."

"Boys - cue the music, roll the credits - we're gonna be rich!"

John 7:53, 8:1-11

Train Up A Child

Jesus asked, "Why do you refuse to obey God's command? The Lord said, 'You must respect your father and mother! If any child says anything bad to their father or mother, he must be put to death!' But you teach that a child can say to their father or mother, 'I have something I could use to help you, but I will give it to God instead.' You are teaching them to not respect their father! So you are teaching that it is not important to do what God said! You are hypocrites!"

Matthew 15:3-7

Prayer Policies

"Whenever you pray, don't be like the hypocrites who always love to pray publicly on street corners and in the synagogues so that everyone can see them. Truly I tell you, they already have their only reward. But whenever you pray, go away by yourself, shut the door behind you, and pray to your Father in secret. Then your Father, who sees all secrets, will reward you. Also, don't babble on and on as people of other religions do."

Matthew 6:5-7

Not In My Father's House!

When He reached Jerusalem, Jesus entered the temple and began to drive out all the people who were buying and selling. He overturned the tables of the money changers and the chairs of those who were selling doves. He stopped everyone from using the Temple as a marketplace and taught, "It is written, 'My house will be called a house of prayer for all nations,' but you have turned it into a den of thieves!" When the head priests heard what Jesus had done, they began planning how to kill Him.

Mark 11:15-18

A Shepherd And His Sheep

"I assure you, I am the gate for the sheep. I am the shepherd of the sheep. I know my sheep. And my sheep know me. I have other sheep too. They are not in this flock here. I must lead them also. In the future there will be one flock and one shepherd. Father says no one takes my life away from me."

Many of the Jews were confused again asking, "Why listen to him? **He is demon-possessed and raving mad!**"

John 10:1-20

Out Of His Mind?

Jesus went back home and a large crowd gathered. It was so large that He and his disciples couldn't find time to eat. When his family heard what he was up to, they went to take custody of Him, saying, **"He has gone insane!"**

Mark 3:20-21

Camp Crusades

"Therefore, go and teach all nations, baptizing them in the name of the Father and the Son and the Holy Spirit. Teach them to obey everything I have commanded you." - *Jesus*

Scripture says, "Whoever believes in him will never be shamed." But how can they call on him to save them unless they believe in him? And how can they believe in him if they have never heard about him? And how can they hear about him unless someone tells them? And how will anyone go and tell them without being sent? That's why the Scriptures say, 'How beautiful are the feet of messengers who bring good news!'" - *Paul*

Matthew 28:19-20, Romans 10:11-15

Service With A Smile

Slaves, obey your human masters with deep fear and respect! Serve them at all times as wholeheartedly as you would serve Christ. Christian slaves should give their masters full respect so God's name and teaching won't be shamed. If your master is a Christian, you should work even harder to help a Christian by your work.

Ephesians 6:5
I Timothy 6:1-2

"I am nothing without Jesus!"

No one can receive anything unless God gives it from heaven. He must become greater and greater, and I must become lesser and lesser. We are of the earth, and we speak of earthly things, but He has come from heaven and is greater than anyone. Those who don't obey the Son will remain under God's angry judgment forever.

Jesus said, "Do not be afraid of those who can only kill your body. I will tell you who to fear - fear the One who can kill you and then throw you into hell for eternity. Yes, He is the One to fear!"

John 3:27-36
Matthew 10:28

Burn The Trash

"I am the vine. You are the branches. If you remain with me, you will produce much fruit. Without me, you can do **nothing** on your own! Without me, you are **useless**, to be thrown away, dried up, gathered into a pile and burned like any other **trash**!" - Jesus, *The Meek and Mild*

John 15:5-6

Keeping Track Of Outcasts

I beg you, keep track of those who cause dissent from the teaching you have learned. Avoid them!

In the name of the Lord Jesus Christ, we command you to keep away from those who are idle, not living within the traditions you have been taught. Take special note of anyone who does not obey this instruction and shun them so that they will be ashamed!

Romans 16:17
2 Thessalonians 3:6,14

Declaring Holy War

Be strong in the Lord's mighty power! Put on the armor of God so that you will be able to withstand the strategies of the devil. We are not fighting against enemies of flesh-and-blood, but against the mighty evil rulers of the dark unseen world, evil spirits in heavenly places. Resist the enemy in the time of evil.

Stand your ground - putting on the belt of truth and the armor of God's righteousness. Put on the shoes of peace. Use the shield of faith to block fiery arrows from the devil. Put on the helmet of salvation and use the sword of the Spirit!

Now is the time to stand alert! Remain firm in the faith - act like men, and be strong!

Ephesians 6:10-17
1 Corinthians 16:13

The Ultimate Privilege

Jesus told his disciples, "He who loves his parents more than Me is not worthy of Me; and he who loves his children more than Me is not worthy of Me.

He who doesn't take up his cross and follow Me isn't worthy of Me. And he who has found his life will lose it! But, he who loses his life - for Me - will find it!"

"Do not fear what you are about to suffer. Be faithful, even if you have to die, and I will give you the crown of eternal life!" - Jesus

Matthew 10:37-39
Revelation 2:10

You. Must. Die.

"Unless a seed falls to the earth and dies, it has no use. The seed has to die to bear fruit. He who loves his own life shall lose it, but he who hates his life in this world will keep it for eternity!" - Jesus Christ, *Prince of Peace*

John 12:24-25

Plausible Prophecy of Pain

The fifth angel blew his trumpet and locusts came out of the smoke. They looked like horses prepared for battle. On their heads they wore a gold crown and on their chests they had iron armor. They had human faces and women's hair. They had the teeth of a lion and tails with stingers like scorpions! The thunder of their wings was like the noise of many horses and chariots hurrying into battle.

They were not allowed to damage the plants, just humans that did not have God's mark on their foreheads. They could not kill, just cause horrible pain like the sting of a scoripon - for five months! Victims will beg to die, but death will never come. The first terror has past. but there are still two more to come!

Revelation 9:1-12

No, what if <u>you're</u> wrong?!?!

Jesus said, "Not everyone who calls me 'Lord' will enter the kingdom of heaven. Many will ask me, 'Lord, did we not prophesy, drive out demons, and perform miracles in your name?' I will look them in the eye and say, 'I never knew you. Get away from me, you evildoers!'"

Peter asked Jesus, "We left everything to follow you. For what?" Jesus said to them, "When the time of the new world comes, everyone who has left their children, brothers, sisters, father, mother, houses, or farms to follow me will receive much more than they left - eternal life!"

All of these people died still believing what God had promised them, but they **never received what was promised**.

Matthew 7:21-23 & 19:27-29
Hebrews 11:13

Omnipotent? Omnipresent? Omnignorant?

God's very first words to humans were about having sex - lots of it. But, isn't it interesting that God's *next words* to Adam turned out to be a lie? Despite the very clear definition of a "day" found in Genesis 1:5, and the clear translation of a physical death (rather than a spiritual one), Adam did not die on *that* day - period. Neither did Eve - she simply became the superstitious scapegoat of a conveniently self-fulfilling prophecy of painful childbirth and the source for all Biblically justified misogynistic treatment of women for every generation to come. (All because of a piece of fruit that God lied about?)

Likewise, doesn't it seem a little odd that God's *very first question* to man in the entire Bible is the result of an all-knowing, all-powerful god's inability to keep track of Adam, His prize creation, the only living man on earth? God's mysterious ways, indeed! It's easy for armchair theologians to suggest, *"God knew where Adam was - he was just acting like any father, giving his son a chance to 'come clean' and accept responsibility."* But, is that what the Bible actually says? How did we come to this evolved theology thousands of years later where Christians believe that God is watching over us at all times, desiring a personal relationship, there for us - morning, noon, and night - watching while we sleep, knowing what we think on our way to work, judging us for coveting our neighbor's lawn when we get home? If God lost Adam, what makes you think He's watching you in the shower?

That said, this first image is a bait and switch, showing an ancient understanding of the earth - complete with the pillars, firmament of heaven, floodgates, and sheol - the dark underworld. It is a seemingly silly segue to a very serious discussion about young earth creationism and its influence on the culture (and currency) of modern times.

"I am a young-age creationist because that is my understanding of the Scripture. If all the evidence in the universe turns against creationism, I would be the first to admit it, but I would still be a creationist because that is what the Word of God seems to indicate." - Dr. Kurt Wise from *In Six Days: Why 50 Scientists Choose to Believe in Creation*, a collection of essays edited by John F. Ashton.

Given Dr. Wise's credentials - earning an M.A. and Ph.D in Geology from Harvard University, I sincerely appreciate his admission of bias as it seems intellectually and ethically honest - especially considering his role as the Director of the Creation Research Center. However, if we can't trust a Ph.D. from Harvard to interpret scientific data without the influence of non-scientific biases, well - who CAN we trust? Let's take a look at how this tradition of relying on the Bible as the *only* science book plays out in American culture today...

46% of Americans hold creationist views on origin of universe - Gallup, Creationism, 2013

46th is where America ranks in science education worldwide. - World Economic Forum, 2013

48% of Americans don't believe in evolution. National Science Foundation (NSF), 2014

26% of Americans believe that the sun revolves around the earth. - NSF, 2014

I share these as examples of hurdles we must overcome if we are to ensure a rational and scientifically literate world for our children and future generations. Indoctrination breeds willful ignorance. This is not just a religious problem, it has become an economic one.

THE DIFFERENCE: True scientists will spend their lives in a pursuit of truth and knowledge. They spend their time hammering their own research, attempting to disprove their own results in order to verify *or* debunk their own theories - all in an humbling quest to uncover the "truth." They often read hundreds of books in their area of expertise and spend a lifetime in the lab - often to only just scratch the surface of a hypothesis at hand. Conversely, a "creation scientist" (like Dr. Wise or Ken Ham) might read a single book in Sunday school as a child and grow up completely convinced that they already have it all figured out. To accept Dr. Wise's premise is to invite a new generation of superstitious and scientifically illiterate society that lacks any curiosity of new discoveries - let alone the ability to think critically for themselves about any data - old or new. The problem with using the Bible as *the* science book isn't heliocentric - it's egocentric.

BONUS: Protecting and promoting this sort of biased ignorance doesn't end with creationism. The same bronze age source of knowledge has been accepted as the "ultimate authority" for everything from parenting to politics. But, we'll get to those subjects a little later...

www.AwkwardMomentsBible.com/FirstOfMany

Giants on Earth?

This illustration was really only intended to be a silly "throw-away" - a passing example of one of the many freak show oddities that appear in the Good Book. Over the centuries, scholars (and conspiracy theorists) have categorized the Nephilim debacle into four main theories: fallen angels, fallen angels who overtook men, the Sethite view, and/or - fallen man. If you are interested, you can find plenty about this subject online. The problem is, only one can be right. Or, quite possibly - none of them are right.

When we first shared this image online, we received an absolute flood of emails claiming everything from "verifiable archaeological proof" of these giants (there is none) to the "correct interpretation of the scripture" (of course, there are many "correct" interpretations that all contradict one another). Here is a snippet from one of my favorite exchanges...

Shirley: The Nephilim were sons of Satan! My pastor says the devil's purpose was to pollute humans to taint the bloodline of Christ so that the seed that God promised would crush him could not be born! The whole purpose of Noah's flood was to exterminate this Satan's mutant race and start all over again with Noah!

Me: One question: Where does the book of Genesis say anything about Satan? Chapter and verse, please?

Shirley: Rev 20:2 and Luke 10:18

Me: Those references are not from Genesis, they were conveniently written about five centuries later - based on the evolved traditions of Jewish storytelling of the Garden of Eden. (Though, I might mention - Revelation still doesn't refer back to "the dragon" as having anything to do with the story in Genesis.) The Bible is actually pretty explicit - Satan is never mentioned in Genesis. As it turns out, sometimes a talking snake is just... a talking snake.

Shirley: WHAT??? Why would Genesis have to explicitly say it was Satan that fathered the Nephilim? CAN'T YOU THINK FOR YOURSELF???

Me: Think? Yes. Fantasize about Satan having sex with humans? No, not my thing, really. Question: Who gets to be on top?

Shirley: On top of what?

www.AwkwardMomentsBible.com/GiantsOnEarth

Dangerous Obedience?

"Don't reason in the mind, just obey in the spirit." from the bestselling *Battlefield of the Mind for Teens*, by Joyce Meyer, one of the most popular mainstream Christian leaders in America today.

While there are more parts of this story (such as the ram in the bush which we illustrated), they all seem quite irrelevant when you consider the main plot points: Abraham heard God's voice asking him to do the unthinkable, Abraham "obeyed in the spirit" without question, and God rewarded him greatly for his obedience. Period.

The question is - what would you be willing to do to obey God? Would you be able to suspend reason (and morality) in order to follow in the footsteps of obedient God-Listeners like Brian David Mitchell, Deanna Laney, Michael Carreiro, Elizabeth Schatz, Zachary Stirewalt, Vince Li, or Jessica Murphy?

Let's move to a more recent case from Jupiter, FL in May of 2014. One day after hearing a church sermon about God's test for Abraham, Kimberly Lucas, a licensed mental health counselor carried out her own reenactment of Genesis 22, testing the Lord by drowning a two year-old girl (and drugging the older brother) before leaving a suicide note that read, *"[the pastor's] sermon really, really touched me yesterday, but God never told me to stop!"*

These are her words, not mine. Of course, most Christian media and blogs immediately denounced any correlation between religion and the tragedy, instead blaming it all on her politics and sexual orientation, throwing out headlines like this one from TrueNewsUSA, *"Obama Supporter & Carpet Munching Lesbian - Kymberly Lucas - charged with murdering her dyke's girlfriend - Jacquelyn Jamason's - two-year-old daughter Elliana - and this lesbo blames the BIBLE!"* (The irony found in the comments section is truly inspiring: *http://bit.ly/1rPT0mz*)

Of course I don't think all religious people are mentally ill and at risk of killing others. The people I mention above are clearly mentally ill, deserving the best help we can give them. However, these cases do beg the question - Which came first? The mental illness, or the religious indoctrination that may have led to it? Yes, random acts of violence happen every day. But, if we are to believe these perpetrator's own words, their psychosis certainly appears to have been

brought on by WANTING to hear God's voice so desperately that they'd do anything... Anything!

OUR POINT? Blindly believing, trusting, and following God's voice can be a slippery slope... Accept Jesus as your personal savior at a teen rally? Great! Strive to be closer to God, learning from the most "righteous" characters in the Bible? Good for you! Cut ties with your family and friends for not being faithful enough? Unfortunate, but biblically justifiable. Slit the throats of your family and friends for being "enemies of God" to prove your obedience when you hear His voice? Suddenly following the voice of God makes you "insane." How convenient.

Some days God's voice might just be advising you on where to go to college because it's the best path toward a brighter future. Other days, He might tell you to kill your children because they are unclean in the eyes of the Lord. If you are taught as a child and conditioned through a lifetime in church to "obey in the spirit" - how would you know where to draw the line? What would you do for God? How could you ever say "no" to the very God you have been trained since childhood to "obey in the spirit?"

ADMISSION: One of my biggest struggles with faith over many years in ministry was that I could never actually "hear God speak" to me in the same way claimed by my colleagues, friends, and family. At times, this made me feel like I was somehow unworthy, and less of a Christian than those who could hear his "voice." In fact, at times it led to outright depression, insomnia, and desperation. *"Why, God? Why are you silent in my life? What do I have to do to get your attention? Answer me, I'll do anything!"* In hindsight, this silence no longer bothers me. It now comforts me as I wonder which of my friends were faking it and which are on a slippery slope to dangerous delusion. Ugh.

www.AwkwardMomentsBible.com/DangerousObedience

WARNING: No Teamwork Allowed!

United in one language? Collaborating as a society? Tapping into your own potential to develop new tools and technologies to make your dreams come true? "AHH, HELL NO!!!" sayeth the Lord.

For all the common claims about the Christian God being a loving, supportive, and nurturing father, you have to admit - this is NOT how most

dads would react when they find their kids working well with others to accomplish something new and interesting to them. No, this is unfortunately how an insecure and abusive father might act at a school science fair - destroying his kid's experiment in front of everyone, just to prove that he's bigger, smarter, and always in control. Some father figure, eh?

"But, but - God destroyed the tower because they were trying to be GREATER than God!" (A common argument.) Really? Is that what the Bible actually says? Choose your favorite translation of Genesis 11:4 and get back to me.

EASTER EGG: No, of course there weren't telescopes back four thousand years ago. However, we thought a little tongue-in-cheek nod to Galileo would be appropriate to illustrate the eerily familiar way in which the church has mimicked God's own actions from this story to divide people, protect ignorance, and impede progress throughout history.

Yet, here we are, thousands of years later, after landing on the moon. Decades later Voyager 1 gracefully exited our solar system thirty-six years after its initial launch - aiming far beyond the heavens they were attempting to reach at Babel. Why no outrage from God this time around? What about the thousands of scientists who have been collaborating for decades on the Large Hadron Collider at CERN, working to unveil more secrets of particle physics including the Higg's Boson, otherwise known as the "God Particle?" What could be more threatening to God? Yet, nothing... silence.

And for that, dear Lord - we thank you.

www.AwkwardMomentsBible.com/NoTeamwork

Daddy Issues

I've always found it odd that Lot became labeled as "righteous" in the Christianity of the New Testament - 2 Peter 2:7. Rrriiigghttt(eous)....

When I talk to my Jewish friends about this, they don't believe he was righteous at all, in fact this story was used to justify the later genocide of the Moabites and the Ammonites - a sort of propaganda of impurity, painting the descendant tribes as the spawn of an *un*righteous man who commits incest with his daughters. (Apparently God let Lot live for other reasons - but, certainly not because he was "righteous.")

So, how exactly did Lot come to be known as a righteous hero of the Old Testament? Need I remind you that this passage comes directly after Lot offers his virginal daughters to be gang-raped by a swarming crowd of townies?

NOW, FOR THE OBVIOUS: I think it's important to note that any man, righteous or otherwise, would have to be VERY drunk to lose sight of the immorality of having sex with his daughters (two nights in a row). So drunk, in fact - that it would be pretty much impossible to achieve the erection, let alone orgasm needed to impregnate his daughters. This logic might lead one to deduce that Lot wasn't as drunk as we are led to believe - enjoying every last... (You get the picture.) Eww.

www.AwkwardMomentsBible.com/IncestIsBest

All Powerful? All Knowing? All Cheating?

Let's forget for a moment that the all-powerful Lord had to cheat in order to win (which He still couldn't do). Let's try to forget that the all-knowing Lord didn't even know Jacob's name (especially considering His plan for Israel). Let's even try to ignore the Lord's own infallible word:

The Lord said, "you can never see my face, for no one can ever see me and live to tell about it!" [Except, of course, for Jacob, Moses, and every single person who sees Jesus walking the earth as "God In The Flesh".] - Exodus 33:20

Okay, I'll admit - I can't ignore any of these things. This epic wrestling match is where Jacob's name is changed to Israel (aka "wrestles with God") and he is blessed by God as the father of the twelve tribes of Israel - a major plot point in the development of Judaism and Christianity. I can't think of another seemingly simple Bible passage that leaves me with more questions about God and the foundations of Judeo-Christian beliefs. At least it gives the basis for another odd dietary rule that prevents Jews from eating the gid hanasheh - the sciatic nerve (or hip).

QUESTION: What do you think God's professional wrestling name would be?

www.AwkwardMomentsBible.com/CheaterCheater

Moses Meets A Magical Bush

When did all of these amazing religious miracles and unquestionable proof of God's existence suddenly cease to exist? Why? I mean, wouldn't everyone on earth just be wowed into submission if a man were able to turn an entire river into blood in the twenty-first century? Heck, I once saw David Blaine levitate! Surely the Lord can top that, right?

Of course, Luke 4:12 answers this question, reminding (warning) us that God is to never be tested. How convenient. (The *Wizard of Oz* could have learned a thing or two from these tricksters.)

Meanwhile I find it interesting how many mainstream Christians are so quick to openly criticize, even mock Mormon's beliefs about Joseph Smith's magic hat, glasses, and golden plates - calling him a con man and a fraud. If you take a step back and think about it critically for a moment, you might realize that the seemingly outlandish claims of Mormonism's central prophet are nothing compared to the alleged magic tricks of Moses.

Likewise, in a similar context, just as modern Christians quickly denounce the claims of Joseph Smith or L. Ron Hubbard as being frauds, the ancient Jews disregarded Jesus as a false prophet, a fake. History just never stops repeating itself...

www.AwkwardMomentsBible.com/MagicBush

No-Choice

"Whether she has or not..." - Numbers 5:14

Remember, ladies - you don't actually have to sin in order to be detained and tortured. It is enough that your husband merely be jealous, suspicious, or insecure enough to give church leaders the right to apprehend you, torture you, and **kill your unborn baby**. In fact, you will even be forced to acknowledge and accept the test as part of your duties as a wife. Pro-Life? No. Pro-Choice? No. No-Choice - the church is in control, under the authority of a loving God.

QUESTION: Is this test somehow magically 100% fool-proof? For example, I wonder how many women were immune to the concoction? Or, was this concoction so powerful that all of the accused were conveniently found guilty (possibly dying from the ritual)? Likewise, the poison would never kill a legitimate child of the accusing husband, would it? I guess that's the real reason there would be no punishment for a husband's false accusations. A sure-fire Catch-22 of a misogynistic culture.

The message to women is quite simple - there is no "choice" involved, and your word means nothing in the eyes of the Lord (or your marriage). The message to husbands is just as clear - if your wife gets pregnant and you don't want to keep the baby, just accuse her of adultery and the church will take care of everything in the name of the Lord.

"But He loves you!" - George Carlin

www.AwkwardMomentsBible.com/NoChoice

A Very Chatty Ass

I never really thought much of this story. Sure, I could recite the standard apologist retorts, but in all honesty, to me, it was always just another allegory using a talking animal - just like any other fable or fairy tale. I wasn't even going to bother with the story until I received the following email:

Barbara: There is no question that the donkey actually spoke to Balaam. God is using this story to illustrate that animals have consciousness and the ability to reason. If God gave the power of speech, He also gave the power to reason because it carried on a two-way rational conversation with Balaam. The story proves that animals have souls and they will be in heaven with us! This is a great comfort to those of us who love our pets.
Me: Do you mind if I ask you a follow-up question? Why don't we see more evangelism being directed toward animals, then? Have you been able to lead your pets to accept Jesus? Are they not required to accept the Lord Jesus Christ as their personal savior? Why the free pass?

Barbara never wrote back. The impressive thing about this story is how a talking donkey suddenly makes a sword-wielding talking angel seem completely plausible - no questions asked. Brilliant!

www.AwkwardMomentsBible.com/ChattyAss

Thirty-Two (Thousand) Virgins

The Lord wasn't a fan of the Midianites, so he told Moses to command his army to slaughter all of them. Well, *almost* all of them...

Much like the modern day Boko Haram in northern Nigeria, Moses' army took the virgins for themselves, to do with as they pleased - turning them into forced brides, sex slaves, or to sell on the black market. Interestingly, God never disciplined Moses or even mentioned the horrible actions against women and children. Instead, the story goes on to explain how the Lord made a deal with Moses to receive an offering of the spoils of war through Eleazar the priest. In the end, 32,000 virgins were captured and divided with the rest of the livestock - 16,000 of the girls were given to the soldiers while the Lord demanded 32 virgins for... Himself!

QUESTION: I always find it interesting how quickly Christians point to Islam and accuse the prophet Muhammed of being a pedophile because of his marriage to Aisha, a nine year-old girl. However, Muhammed was a man. **God is God.** What exactly did God do with these 32 virgins?

www.AwkwardMomentsBible.com/32Virgins

More Than A Woman

Oh, calm down, calm down! We're not implying anything with this illustration! We are simply combining all of the passages that specifically refer to David and Jonathan's special "relationship" (found in 1 Samuel and 2 Samuel) into a single narrative. The rest of those books of the Bible are all about wars and King Saul trying to find and kill young David, the son of their servant, who was knit to the soul of the son of the king.

Sure, it might be the making of an epic love story of star-crossed lovers, but - we're not saying there was anything questionable about their bro-mance! Boys will be boys, right? Though, *if* a movie were

ever to be made, I'd expect it to be a musical, titled *Shame!*, starring Neil Patrick Harris and Nathan Lane who perform the Bee Gees' *More Than A Woman* under the experienced direction of Ang Lee.

After all of the (still to be deciphered) hate-mail we received for "promoting the LGBT agenda" with our first book, I'd just like to remind readers that we didn't make this all up - it's in the Bible.

For those interested, the references to kissing one another until David "exceeded" is directly out of the King James Version - 1 Samuel 20:41

www.AwkwardMomentsBible.com/MoreThanAWoman

The Kid Gets It

This illustration has been a long time in the making. I'll never forget hearing this story in church for the first time when I was in college, shortly after becoming "born again." At the time, I was also slightly obsessed with gangster movies - from the classics like *The Godfather* and *Goodfellas* to more modern takes on the genre like *Pulp Fiction* and *Reservoir Dogs*.

One theme you pick up on early is that if you want to really control a person that might be of use to you later, don't threaten them personally, but go after their family. Don't wanna pay the bribe? Your wife loses a finger. Do something to undermine a leader's authority? Your baby mysteriously dies in his crib that night. You've been warned, *"Do not f*** with 'the family!'"* Of course, David takes his punishment and lives on, richly blessed by God for his obedience. The son God killed? What son?

Suddenly it hit me, God is the most intimidating mob boss out there. Isn't it interesting how this same methodology has been passed down through the ages by the church? One generation after another? Just think about the Catholic Church for a moment. The hierarchy. The business structure. The corruption. The coercion. It is no mistake - they are just following in their Father's footsteps, taking care of the family business.

God works in mysterious ways? His ways are beyond our understanding? No He doesn't, no they aren't. According to the Bible, it is quite simple.

EASTER EGG: In the family portrait on the wall, the chair is not actually empty...

www.AwkwardMomentsBible.com/TheKidGetsIt

A Whore No More

Since our first book was released, I found myself conflicted, at odds with fans who begged us to illustrate the first part of this story. Honestly, I never had any interest in discussing the genitals and emissions of barnyard animals. It just seemed too easy, too low-brow. However, the content that follows is a cautionary tale that is quite captivating.

No, no - this story is not really about two sisters. It is written as an allegorical warning against the kingdoms of Samaria and Jerusalem, to warn of their punishments for turning away from God. Although, isn't it interesting how the explicit language chosen certainly appears to be indicative of how female idolaters, adulterers, and prostitutes were treated back in the day. How else would this prescription of unthinkable torture find its way into the literature of the Old Testament if there was not already a culturally relatable (acceptable) understanding that God's punishment of a wayward nation might be just as horrific as the justified punishment of a common impure street whore?

Now, if you can stomach it, imagine this scene. Just imagine the blood-curdling screams as her ears were cut off without mercy. Imagine the terror as she was endlessly gang raped by her enemies. Imagine the panic and humiliation as she was forced to drink the same poison as her sister. Close your eyes and imagine being held down at all limbs as your attackers use brutal force and a dull knife to saw through the skin and cartilage to remove your nose. Imagine being so desperate for your own death that you give in to demands to rip off your own breasts with your bare hands. Imagine watching your own children being murdered with swords right in front of you before your only prayer is answered - your own death.

Just imagine all of the horrors that have been, and will continue to be justified by the conveniently irreputable will of an all-loving, merciful, forgiving Father that shares the almighty throne with His son, our Lord and Savior - Jesus Christ, the Prince of Peace. You don't have to imagine - just do a keyword search in Google News to find the daily local stories that never make national headlines.

www.AwkwardMomentsBible.com/WhoreNoMore

The Necromancer

I'll admit - some Bible stories are just fun to illustrate. Especially the passages that resemble the colorful acid-trip musical dream sequences that once appeared in the middle of old Disney films. I wonder, whatever happened to those interludes? Wait! Now I wonder what the heck happened to Ezekiel's amazing bone army?

www.AwkwardMomentsBible.com/BoneArmy

Bad Human, Bad!

No, no - not everything in the Bible is about rape, murder, incest, racism, and misogyny. Some passages are just light-hearted fun or even quite instructional! After all, isn't this where we get the idea of potty training dogs by rubbing their noses in *it*? To me, this story certainly says a lot about how God sees his "children" on earth.

Isn't it funny how churches will gladly exploit the very next chapter of Malachi to preach all about the importance of tithing properly but conveniently forget to mention this lovely passage? Of course, it's likely no coincidence that a story about tithing directly follows a grim reminder of God's demeaning intimidation tactics, designed to ensure ongoing compliance (and that beautiful jingle-jangle sound of 10% hitting the collection plate every Sunday). Pay up, suckers - remember the dung!

Meanwhile, according to a recent study by Pew Research, there are currently over 2 billion Christians who choose to worship this dung-flinging deity. Though, in their defense, they've likely never been exposed to this particular passage of God's unending love in their "studies."

Personally, I could never train a dog this way. But, then again – I'm merely human. Who am I to question the Lord? (Someone who does his best to never abuse his authority over man or beast.)

www.AwkwardMomentsBible.com/PottyTraining

Keeping Score

As we transition from the Old Testament to the New Testament, I think it is important to take a moment and reflect on an important claim that Jesus made about Himself:

"I and my Father are one." John 10:30 (KJV)
"Verily, verily, I say unto you, Before Abraham was, I am." John 8:58 (KJV)

Most Christians would characterize Jesus as the patient, all-loving, compassionate "Prince of Peace." In the next breath, they might remind you that Jesus (the Son) was quite literally God (the Father), here on earth – in the flesh. These two, along with the Holy Spirit have always been one and the same – what is referred to as The Trinity. You can't separate them. To do so is to throw out the very basis of monotheistic Christianity.

Many believe that New Testament scriptures like those referenced above solidify the position of Jesus (The Son) as an equal partner of the Trinity. However, this presents some problems for the "meek and mild" Jesus of modern interpretation. On the other hand, when you reverse the transitive properties of the Trinity, bringing the characteristics of the jealous, angry, murderous God from the Old Testament forward into the New Testament - it actually helps. Suddenly some of the most confusing and problematic passages of Jesus' life make much more sense - no longer requiring the most authentic scriptures to be hidden in the footnotes while centuries of apologists scramble to explain "what Jesus really meant" whenever He acts "out of character" (or, at least, out of His folklorish caricature that has evolved over centuries).

By contrast, I had one of my most profound moments of confusion (even crisis) as a Christian when I came to the realization that Satan wasn't nearly as bad of a guy as modern traditions have come to suggest. The uncomfortable truth of the matter is, when it comes to Biblical rap sheets, the little red guy with the pitchfork is a minor, powerless street thug compared to the genocidal warlord that monotheistic Christians have come to adore - The Trinity®.

According to Steve Wells' excellent book, *Drunk with Blood: God's Killings in the Bible* - the score isn't even close. God (aka Jesus): 2,821,364 murdered. Satan: 10 (Poor Job's family - and even then, only under God's blessing as part of a sadistic bet). Was it Satan that threw a temper tantrum and flooded the entire earth, killing his own creation? Was it Satan who killed all of the unicorns in Isaiah and all of the firstborn in Exodus? Was it Satan who kept 32 virgins for himself? No. According to Jesus, *"Before Abraham was, I am. I and my Father are one."*

POOR SATAN: He doesn't even have the power to cast souls into hell. That privilege, my friends, belongs to the One and Only - the sweet, gentle, and innocent - little Lord Jesus, asleep on the hay.

www.AwkwardMomentsBible.com/KeepingScore

No Damsel, No Distress

"Let he who is without sin cast the first stone…"
This has always been one of my favorite Bible stories - full of compassion, courage, and conviction. It is truly one of the most dramatic examples of Jesus' morality and worthiness as a leader of men. I don't think a day goes by that someone doesn't quote this verse on our Facebook page as a way of reminding us not to judge others. Unfortunately, there is a problem: **it's not actually Biblical.**

Contrary to popular belief, the Bible did not just appear out of thin air one day. It was hand-crafted over many centuries by many different men with many different audiences and agendas. Eventually, councils of men (who, like the authors of the books in question, had no first-hand knowledge of the life of Jesus) were formed to decide which of these writings were worthy of being part of the canon. Many books were tossed out, some sought out, in order to establish what we now consider the Holy Bible, the Good Book, the Word of God!

However, the editing didn't stop with the councils. Rulers, priests and lowly scribes have always had a hand in massaging the text to fit the needs of the day. Don't like the way Jesus got angry with a leper for asking to be healed? Easy - just change one word from 'anger' to 'compassion.' Suddenly notice that there is no explicit mention of the trinity anywhere in the original Greek texts?

Simple - just convince a scholarly pawn of the powerful church to add it to the next version in the 1500s. Need a dramatic story to show Jesus as a hero in the face of authority, saving a poor girl from the hands of the wicked Pharisees? Well, that brings us to this interesting passage - the *Pericope Adulterae*. (John 7:53, 8:1-11)

There are very few scholars who believe the story of Jesus saving the adulterous woman to be authentic - for many reasons. First and foremost, **it doesn't exist** in the oldest, most authentic manuscripts. That's right - it is simply not found in the original copies of the Gospel of John. Second, the style of writing and language is quite noticeably different from the rest of the Gospel of John. Third, it is somewhat sloppily inserted right in the middle of the story of the Feast of the Tabernacles that begins with John 7:1 before being abruptly cut off by the Pericope Adulterae, eventually to resume again with John 8:12 through 9:7.

But, let's get back to the first point: it doesn't exist anywhere in the oldest manuscripts! It does appear in the *Codex Benzae* from the 5th century, what I often refer to as Bible 2.0, a manuscript filled with other oddities; the longer ending to the book of Mark, the complete absence of John 5:4, and the book of Acts being considerably longer than other manuscripts of the day. Even alongside the Codex Benzae were other manuscripts that explicitly questioned the validity of this passage. This leads us to ask many questions:

1. Who added it centuries later and why?

2. If we know that it was added much later, why is it still in the Bible?

3. Why do only a few Bibles include a tiny footnote that says, *"Some manuscripts do not include this passage?"*

4. Why do the majority of churches still teach this as a major story in the ministry of Jesus?

5. What other parts of the Bible were added by scribes and rulers after the canon was formed?

But, most of all - why do Christians love to quote this story anytime it might help them avoid the judgment of others, yet remain completely unaware of the considerable problems with its authenticity? All of these questions are worth asking.

SIDE NOTE: For those who might argue, "But there was probably a good reason that it was removed from the earliest and most authentic manuscripts - they didn't want it to look like Jesus was permissive of adultery," I'd ask - isn't that the same problem? Letting man decide what is *really* God's word because of the *wants* of the day?

www.AwkwardMomentsBible.com/NoDamselNoDistress

To ~~Train~~ Abuse & Murder A Child

Now that we've gotten one of the most blatant additions to the Bible out of the way, let's take a look at a story that appears to be quite authentic to the earliest, most original versions of scripture.

"Jesus obviously isn't telling people to kill their children! He's being sarcastic to show the Pharisees their hypocrisy for focusing on one particular law but not another... He was just kidding!" - Cassie J.

While the idea of a sarcastic jokester Jesus is quite entertaining, I can't find any other instances where He exhibits this particular personality trait. Not to mention - being sarcastic about *His* own laws that *He* cast down through the prophets? This seems quite improbable, especially after going out of His way back in Matthew 5:18 to reiterate that *"not one letter, not one iota of the law shall pass away."*

This story continues as Jesus tells His disciples that the Pharisees are "blind" for worrying about washing their hands while they eat, but they should be pure of heart, to fend off evil thoughts, murder, adultery, sexual immorality, theft, lying, and slander. But, do we really think Jesus suspected that the Pharisees, the ultra-strict religious leaders of the Jews would actually condone such things? Of course not! This leads us back to Jesus' reminder of His own law's penalty for disobedient children.

So, what would Jesus do? How would He want us to raise our kids? According to Proverbs 22:6 which led to Michael and Debi Pearl's bestselling Christian parenting book, *To Train Up A Child*, it might involve rubber tubing to invoke horrible pain while evading visible detection by authorities. (That is, of course, if the child lives to tell anyone...)

But, what if Cassie was right? What if Jesus was just being sarcastic? Try telling that to 13 year-old Hana Williams who died in her own back yard on May 11, 2011. Her head shaved, her malnourished naked body face-down in the cold mud, no longer shaking from hypothermia - all as her mother watched from inside the home, following the book's advice to not reward any of her "attention seeking behavior." According to court records, her mother eventually called 911 to report, *"I think my daughter just killed herself. She's really rebellious."*

Tragically, Hana was not the first, nor will she be the last. The authors of *To Train Up A Child* report over 600,000 copies of the parenting manual have been sold, bringing their "ministry" millions of dollars in... blood money. It is important to note, Hana's parents were **only caught once there was a body to dispose of**. Others continue the abuse...

"If any child says anything bad to their father or mother, they must be put to death!"
- Jesus Christ, Matthew 15:4

More victims and quotes from TTUAC online:
www.AwkwardMomentsBible.com/ToTrainUpAChild

36 U.S.C. § 119 - Est. 1952

Let's move on to one of the more rebellious acts of an out-of-work carpenter who often ruffled the feathers of the leaders of the day. Imagine for a moment that you are a pastor, standing before your congregation, praying publicly for God to bless this, to fix that, etc... Suddenly a complete stranger storms in - shouting insults, demanding you follow his own rules, condemning your religious practices.

Would the church take kindly to such a rebuke? Not likely. Now, just imagine the same scene in an era of almost unchecked power of the religious leaders back in Jesus' day. He made the naughty list!

Through a series of serendipitous travel mishaps, I found myself in Washington D.C. this spring. Agnes is not an American but just happened to be seeing clients in the area so we arranged to meet at a coffee shop just a block from the National Mall. When I walked in, she was visibly excited - asking what was going on, why it seemed so busy, why there were so many protesters on the streets holding dramatic signs demanding everything from bans on abortion and gay marriage to the inclusion of prayer and creationism in public schools. Then it dawned on me - it was the first Thursday in May. The National Day Of Prayer, a national religious holiday invented by the U.S. Congress and ratified into law via 36 U.S.C. § 119 back in 1952. A law written 161 years after our very First Amendment promised freedom of religion... Or lack thereof?

Earlier that morning, President Barack Obama did his legal duty by issuing an annual proclamation required by another public law 100-307, ending his otherwise abstract invocation with the final words, *"I join all people of faith in asking for God's continued guidance, mercy, and protection as we seek a more just world."*

Of course, this is quite the departure from the first proclamation issued in 1952 by Harry Truman: *"Whereas from the earliest days of our history our people have been accustomed to turn to **Almighty God** for help and guidance... I deem it **fitting** that this **Day of Prayer** coincide with the anniversary of the adoption of the Declaration of Independence, which published to the world this Nation's 'firm reliance on the protection of **Divine Providence**...'*

*[I] do hereby proclaim Friday, July 4, 1952, as a **National** Day of Prayer, on which all of us, in our churches, in our homes, and in our hearts, may beseech **God** to grant us wisdom to know the course which we should follow, and strength and patience to pursue that course steadfastly. May we also give thanks to **Him** for **His** constant watchfulness over us in every hour of national prosperity..."*

Fitting? On the 4th of July? America's day of celebrating independence from, among other things, the state sponsored Church of England? Make no mistake - given his history of labeling America as a "Christian Nation," Truman is not inviting people of *all* faiths to join in prayer - just the Christians. This, in a time when it was seen as blatantly un-American and un-patriotic to not bow your head in prayer whenever expected to do so.

QUESTION: Where else do national leaders call out from the halls of power for citizens to unite in a religious endeavour? Iran, perhaps?

I should point out that the primary organizing body, the National Day of Prayer Task Force, is a private Christian non-profit organization out of Colorado. However, their patriotic logo and excellent marketing campaigns certainly give an air of "official business" to the countless Americans who might be heard boasting, "America is a Christian nation! If you don't like it, get the f*ck out!" In short, the day is a big deal as tens of thousands of churches and partner groups come out across the country to join together in a public prayer that is broadcast from the taxpayer-owned Canon Office Building (between the Capitol Building and the Library of Congress), featuring Christian celebrities like Anne Graham Lotz (daughter of Rev. Billy Graham) and Dr. James Dobson (of Focus on the Family fame). The official verse for 2014 was taken from the Christian New Testament, Romans 15:6, *"So that with one mind and one voice you may glorify the God and Father of our Lord Jesus Christ."*

According to an April 8, 2014 press release,

"The theme for the 2014 National Day of Prayer, is One Voice, United in Prayer, emphasizing the need for individuals to join together in corporate prayer, calling upon the unfailing character of God, who is sovereign over all governments, authorities, and men – the God under whom this nation stands." So much for praying in private, eh?

We chose to illustrate a satirical perspective on the National Day of Prayer, putting the President on the steps of the Capitol Building at a massive rally. This did not happen. In fact, quite the opposite! In 2009 and again in 2010, gullible Christians **lost their minds** when hoax emails were circulated, claiming, *"This year President Obama canceled the 21st annual National Day of Prayer ceremony at the White House under the ruse of 'not wanting to offend anyone'."* - going on to spread all sorts of blatant propaganda about Obama being a Muslim, holding Islamic prayers at the White House, etc... I received the chain email from at least 15 *very angry* people.

IN OTHER NEWS: A 2014 study from Pew Research shows that "atheism" would be the worst negative against a candidate from potential voters in the upcoming 2016 elections - regardless of professional or political qualifications. In fact, a lack of belief in God was TWICE as damaging to a candidate as homosexuality or marijuana use. 70% of Republicans said they wouldn't be willing to support an atheist candidate, while "only" 43% of Democrats would hold a person's *lack* of faith against them. In short, if you don't believe in God, you have no place in government. More clearly stated, if you don't openly SAY that you believe in God, you can't get elected.

QUESTION: I wonder if any politician has ever told a lie to get elected? Nah.

www.AwkwardMomentsBible.com/PrayerInPublic

The Money Changers

There's a reason we illustrated this passage in a modern context. Just imagine if a trouble-making demon-possessed "false prophet" were to storm into a megachurch and threaten the livelihoods of modern church leaders? Now, what if this occurred back in a day without camera phones and 24-hour investigative journalism - when religious leaders had all of the power and wanted to keep it that way?

Megachurch pastor Joel Osteen may be able to avoid the wrath of God by technically not taking a salary from the largest church in America today. Yet, his net worth still weighs in at over $40 million thanks to product sales to his Christian audience. In March of 2014, Osteen's Lakewood Church (which spent $105 million dollars renovating the former Houston Rockets stadium as its new home for its 40,000 members) lost over $600,000 in offerings stolen from one day of services. And that's just the cash and checks! (Direct deposit and credit card tithes were not affected. Praise the Lord!)

Differences aside, Pat Robertson is a truly brilliant businessman, no stranger to making money off fellow Christians. Originally an active ordained Southern Baptist minister, I wonder if Robertson felt threatened by this story of Jesus punishing the money changers and decided to take his business outside the walls of the church. Between launching the top-rated Christian Broadcasting Network (CBN), the Christian Coalition, and Regent University, it is hard to imagine how he found the time to write so many bestselling books while also hosting his live Christian TV show, *The 700 Club*. Always an opportunist, even the planes used by his relief organization Operation Blessing somehow found their way to deliver equipment to his diamond mines in Zaire during the Rwandan genocide crisis - truly impressive planning and logistics! According to a Wikipedia source, Robertson's net worth is estimated to be anywhere between $200 Million and $1 Billion. (Unfortunately, 'Mr. Pat,' his $520,000 thoroughbred race horse was not as successful.)

Don't worry about Joyce Meyer - she is reportedly only worth about $25 Million, barely enough to cover the private jet that shuttles her between luxurious homes around the country. I'm sure that the only reason the IRS and U.S. Senate investigated her ministry's financials was because of... the devil! (Note: While she might be the most successful female Christian leader and Bible teacher in America today, she apparently has no interest in following *all* scripture. Say, 1 Timothy 2:12?)

As a capitalist pig myself, I guess I don't actually have a problem with these Christian leaders making money off of their businesses - just their tax-free megachurches (aka tax-shelters). The simple fact of the matter is, these leaders are nothing in the grand scheme of Religionomics. From the sale of every VeggieTales video to the receipt of every tax free tithe, Christianity is a HUGE multi-billion dollar business. Don't take my word for it - just check out the banner advertising on BibleGateway.com, the most popular online Bible engine. Now owned by

Zondervan Publishing (a division of Harper Collins), the Bible publisher is making millions off of banner advertising for everything from expensive Christian colleges to Christian dating sites like ChristianMingle.com. That's right, folks - blatant solicitations for hook-up sites, right there in the middle of the Word of God! What would Jesus do?

www.AwkwardMomentsBible.com/TheMoneyChangers

Demon Possessed?

In the spirit of full disclosure - the only way to fit this long-winded, repetitive, and fairly incoherent story onto one page was to summarize it. A lot.

Why would the Jewish leaders think Jesus was "demon possessed and raving mad?" Would it be, perhaps, because He was rambling on and on like any false prophet would, given a busy street corner and a megaphone?

If you've ever visited a big city, you've likely encountered various street performers - musicians, mimes, even elaborate pop-up puppet shows - all attempting to get their piece of the action from charitable tourists. Some of these performers are ridiculously talented, while others are just... ridiculous. There are those who appear quite professional and lucid, while others carry on incoherently, creating an invisible forcefield that magically causes passersby to avoid any eye contact while crossing the street as quickly as possible - grumbling, "what a nutjob" under their breath.

But, who did these Jewish leaders think they were? Accusing this man of being demon posessed and raving mad? They barely even knew him - it's not like they were members of his own family or anything! (Next illustration, please...)

www.AwkwardMomentsBible.com/RavingMad

Insane In The Membrane

I imagine most Christians would find any question of Christ's sanity to be "insane" in and of itself. Not to mention - blasphemous and personally insulting. Therein lies the challenge - **complete strangers** separated by centuries, assuming that they would know better than a man's **own family**...

This isn't the only time the Bible refers to Jesus as being something other than the perfect Son of God. In fact, the very next passage begins with the townspeople accusing Jesus of being possessed by Beelzebul, the ruler of demons. And, why wouldn't they believe this?

Try putting these stories into a modern perspective. If you found yourself on a subway train when a stranger came aboard (along with his gang) and began preaching to passengers that: not only was he the Son of God, but God himself - AND that the only way to get to heaven was through him - AND that you needed to abandon your family to follow him - AND that you needed to drink his blood and eat his flesh for eternal life.... Would you move *closer* to this man and his ragtag group of followers and ask for more information? Of course not! You'd treat him like any other insane person. At first, you might try to politely ignore him. Eventually you might call the cops and hope the mental health department could handle things.

Now, imagine this was YOUR OWN son or brother. Your heart would be breaking! You would be terrified, trying to protect him, trying to get him any help you could!

Yes, this is horribly sad and any parent can imagine the very helpless terror of poor Mary, as she watched her son carry his cross to his own death, clearly unaware of the reality of his own fate. Yet, this gut-wrenching sadness does not a deity make. Many mothers have watched their mentally ill children suffer and die horrific deaths, often unaware of what was even happening to them as the needle was placed in their arm or the noose tied around their neck. Tragic. Horrific. 100% Human.

But, this story doesn't stop at verse 21 as Jesus' family continues to reach out to Him:

Then His mother and His brothers arrived. standing outside they called for Him. A crowd was sitting around Him, and they said to Him, "Your mother and Your brothers are outside looking for You." Jesus answered, "Who are My mother and My brothers?" Looking at those who were sitting around Him, Jesus said, "You are My mother and My brothers! Whoever does the will of God is My brother and sister and mother."
Mark 3:31-35

IMPORTANT QUESTIONS: Are these not the words and actions of any "insane" cult leader who would abandon everything to live out their own obsession, acting out their delusion? Can we really take the disciples' word for what *really* happened in the New Testament, when, by following this leader, they may have been just as "insane" themselves? When brainwashed followers are rescued from cults like Jonestown, Heaven's Gate or the Branch Davidian - do we take their bizarre claims about living on comets seriously? Of course not! Their families know they're mentally ill.

OTHER TRANSLATIONS: Some versions of the Bible say that His family thought Jesus was "crazy" or had "gone mad" or was "out of his mind." Either way, if it quacks like a duck...

www.AwkwardMomentsBible.com/Insanity

Camp Crusades

I fully understand that my next sentence may upset some well-meaning people and I'm okay with that. In short, Christian "missions" are often the summer camp equivalent of the Crusades - simply replacing swords with bottled water while expecting the same result. In the 21st century, this has become the ultimate Christian vacation experience - saving the world, one tour bus stop at a time.

It is one thing to provide food, water, clothing, and medicine - and there are thousands of relief workers across the globe doing this important and noble work. However, it is quite another to expect the recipients to denounce their history, culture, customs, and even their health in exchange. That is an evangelistic bait-and-switch game of cultural genocide. Does religion really equal relief?

This, I might add, coming from a man who spent much of his life involved with international missions and continues to support effective critical needs relief work, regardless of the religious leanings of the operating organization. I am not saying that some missionaries don't do great work - after all, life-saving vaccines and water purification plants know no religion. I'm just concerned by the motivations with which they do this work and the expectations in return. Unfortunately, many of the full-time missionaries I know are quite blind to the impending extinction of cultural diversity brought forth in the name of God (aka western capitalism). As long as they accept Christ, what else matters?

"Be more like me and the world will be a better place. Here is your water and your Bible, we'll see you

in a couple of hours for an exciting message from Pastor Dan. After the story time, we'll be feeding everyone dinner and we'll be singing some songs. You are hungry, aren't you? Please join us. Let us pray..."

Again, there are many organizations that do *truly amazing* aid work, at home and abroad. However, those NGO's don't usually keep track of how many hands are raised during the worship and prayer service that follows an open-air film presentation about spending a fiery eternity in hell if you don't raise your hand. This, all in order to show donors how many souls they've saved as a result of their ongoing donations. If you believed the sum of all the missions reports, you'd see every inhabitant of Africa has been "saved" several times already.

This is also where the summer camp equivalency comes into play, giving Christians a chance to play missionary tourist for a couple of weeks to really feel the power of the Holy Spirit at work. In certain parts of the world, the locals have been conditioned to show up every time the missionaries arrive - to put on a little show of local customs, accept the water, eat the food, listen to the same story from the same man, raise the same hand, receive another Bible, have their pictures taken, and go back to their lives... The next weekend, missionaries go home feeling like they've made a huge difference in the world - so much better than a weekend at Disneyland! My point? There is a fine line between missional evangelism and crusade tourism, exploiting what I refer to as "poverty porn."

COMMONALITY: I have been involved in several missions filled with as many glammed-out millionaires as born-again college students - all seeking a life-changing experience that might give meaning to *their* lives, playing the part of God's chosen missionary - complete with their photos next to starving orphans to prove... What? To whom?

I'm still a huge supporter of many humanitarian organizations, many of which are Christian. However, looking back through my own history in the field, I am now ashamed by some of the work that I was a part of. As a result, I now stand in firm opposition to groups whose primary function is to evangelize the "savages" by seeking out "untouched" indigenous peoples who keep to themselves. They are encouraged to put on western clothes, eat western food, pose for western pictures, and establish a western sense of "order" while rejecting any non-Christian values or beliefs. All, while receiving new western diseases (to which there is no local immunity) and yes, at times - even having their kids kidnapped to provide a "better life" with Jesus back home. Evangelism? No.

www.AwkwardMomentsBible.com/CampCrusades

Slaves, Obey Your Masters

During a missions trip to Ghana, I found myself on a beautiful beach on the Gulf of Guinea one morning. I was surrounded by a swarm of bustling women and children who waved goodbye to all the men as they pushed their small fishing boats out through the breaking waves in hope of a good day's catch. The sand was white, the sky was blue, the sun was warm, yet - I couldn't help looking over my shoulder at the ominous reminder of a horrific not-so-distant past - the towering Elmina Castle, a major hub in the Atlantic slave trade.

Later that day I found myself struggling to hear any of the words coming out of the guide's mouth. On the verge of tears for over an hour, I thought back to a trip to Auschwitz years earlier. Something about this castle seemed more insidious to me. Why was it so different? As I stood inside the largest cell, the darkness barely lit by a single barred doorway far at one end, I heard the only words I remembered from that day, "600 men and 400 women."

What? In here? All at once? The cell was no larger than an elementary classroom! Then it hit me - this place was so different from Auschwitz because these prisoners were expected to *live*! This wasn't death row, it was an assembly line.

Lingering back to hide my tears behind my camera, I took this photo of... Darkness.

That evening, I found myself back on the same beach, trying to enjoy an amazing sunset for which the Gold Coast is known. Instead, I prayed:

*What kind of a God would issue a commandment against coveting another man's property but **not** against making another human being a piece of property in the first place? What kind of loving*

God stands by as millions of His own children are bought, sold, and slaughtered - justified by the laws given by His own Word and Law? What kind of Son of God would allow the father of the early church to utter a phrase such as: *'Slaves, obey your masters...'*

So, there I was - a mere human, knowing full well that owning another human has always been morally wrong. Meanwhile, my colleagues were out distributing Bibles that prescribed and promoted the very atrocities that Elmina Castle was built to facilitate. Looking back, as I sat on that beach with tears again filling my eyes, it may have been one of the final nails in the coffin of my Christianity.

www.AwkwardMomentsBible.com/SlavesObey

"I am NOTHING without Jesus!"

Originating from a culture obsessed with sin and brokenness, sayings like this continue to infect the collective Christian consciousness through a steady stream of everything from self-annihilating Sunday sermons to sadly ironic bumper stickers, t-shirts and internet memes. Proof of this self-loathing has become a badge of honor of sorts - viewed, liked, shared, and re-shared every day by some of the most popular Christian pages online, like Facebook's *Jesus Daily* with over 25 million fans who reply with their own ironically nihilistic refrains:

I am broken.
I am worthless.
I am weak.
I am nothing.

This is selficide. Are there any mantras more deplorable, more dehumanizing or more damaging to the human psyche than those flippantly tossed about in everyday conversation from one believer to another? To speak, somehow joyfully, of a life without meaning or worth? Is there a more harmful message for our children, spouses, or neighbors? If you repeat these words often enough, they are bound to become true. Is it any great surprise that there appears to be a strong correlation between Christian culture and the number of self-help titles lining the shelves of local bookstores?

Of course, Christians normally add the awe-inspiring "without Jesus" to the end of these phrases, somehow making them... What, better?

Less harmful? Less meaningful? No! The very first requirement of Christianity is to believe that you are weak and worthless, - a broken sinner. How else would you be completely wowed by a savior that would die just for you? *Worthless, pathetic you!* If you aren't convinced that you have a disease, what's the point in looking for a cure? (Of course, threats of a wrathful God and eternal damnation doesn't hurt.)

Unfortunately, it is actually Jesus who wants you to become "lesser and lesser" to begin with! To bow at His feet, to cower in His presence - just like His Father. Though, somehow Jesus (God 2.0) is much better at making you believe that it's all your fault to begin with. Personally. Sure, He has come to save you - *just* as long as you first agree how great He is and admit just how insignificant and guilty you are! It's your fault that He had to die on that cross! He is greater, you are lesser, it's your fault. Period.

Now that almost seven years have passed since I left full-time ministry, my thoughts have become clearer and I find it quite difficult to imagine the true psychological harm that I helped inject into otherwise happy lives - all under the guise of sharing the "Good News" - spreading mixed messages laced with heavy doses of sinfulness, brokenness, bigotry, hatred, worthlessness, superstition, and divine intuition. Of course, this was always quite subversive, certainly never intentional - the real focus being on leading people to *better* life through Christ! These people didn't know what they were missing! They didn't realize how broken they were! They needed Jesus to save them! He loved them, no matter what! *(Next illustration, please...)*
www.AwkwardMomentsBible.com/IAmNothing

Burn The Useless Garbage!

Geezus, Jesus - tell us how you really feel! When I first wrote online about the mantra, "I am NOTHING without Jesus!" many argued:

```
"You are blowing this completely out of
proportion! Mainstream Christianity would
never teach such a vile philosophy and
there is no Biblical basis for your
slander against our Lord Jesus!" - Barb J.
```

Really? This passage seems to sum it all up in the words of Jesus Himself. Like Father, like Son.
www.AwkwardMomentsBible.com/BurnTheTrash

One Nation, Under Vishnu

I recently found myself in a friendly argument with two old friends from Tulsa and Boise. They were both very upset over a lawsuit in New Jersey that was challenging the "**under God**" insertion be taken back out of the pledge of allegiance in the public school setting. For them, it was all about *"the traditional pledge of a Christian nation,"* further asserting that, "atheists are forcing their beliefs on others!" Even as a devout Christian, I always found the addition of "Under God" to the pledge to be a much more complex issue than most of my fellow Christian friends were willing to admit. As such, I welcomed the opportunity for a very interesting dialogue, shedding a little light on how many Americans (who happen to live in predominantly Christian communities) may have lost sight of the history, legality, and social importance of the issue.

I took my friends on a little journey, encouraging them to imagine how many kids in a New Jersey school might be Hindu, Buddhist, Muslim, Jewish, Scientologist, or - Lord forbid - agnostic or atheist. I invited them to think outside of their own communities to remember that New Jersey is much more of a cultural melting pot than their hometowns. Then I asked them to imagine the circumstances under which some of those families might have recently fled countries with mandated state-sponsored religion. I asked them to imagine escaping in the middle of the night to find yourself in the "Land of the Free," only to be told that, in order to become a citizen, you must first publicly recite a national pledge that includes reference to the national deity of the majority religion. As an added bonus, their children will also be required to recite the pledge every morning. In public school. In front of their peers and authority figures. Under God... (No, really - think about that for a moment...)

For me, the case in New Jersey is not about taking "under God" out of the pledge, it is about taking it *back out*... Both of my friends come from a generation that is under the impression that "under God" was just always part of the pledge. They had no idea that it was added back in 1954 by President Eisenhower (who had been baptized as a born-again Christian just a year earlier) in the midst of the Cold War, as a way to distinguish

America from the "atheist communists" around the world - in an era of Joseph McCarthy's list-making paranoia where almost anything could get you blacklisted as un-American and ostracized by society. Talk about "forcing beliefs"?!?!

KEEPING TRACK: I went on to suggest that the New Jersey lawsuit wasn't about forcing atheist beliefs on anyone. To me, it was about parents who didn't want to have their own kids ostracized for not publicly accepting the presence of the "majority god's" watchful eye over the country - avoiding the beliefs of others being forced on *their own kids*.

Many proponents of the "under God" addition might argue, *"Fine, then just don't have your kid say, 'under God' if you don't like it!"* I might have to argue that it is not quite as simple as instructing young dissenting students to silently omit the phrase in a classroom full of their peers and authority figures without fear of prejudice, while others chant, "under God" in unison. In many classrooms, this silence would be quite noticeable, tipping your hat to a *different* belief system, forcing children (or adults) to publicly "out" themselves as going against the status quo - an outsider, one who should be *shunned and shamed* according the Bible.

Now, please take a moment to go back and re-read the Bible verses we chose for this illustration and think about it critically for a moment...

Is it really that difficult to imagine a public school teacher, who happens to be a Christian, subconsciously (or even very consciously) keeping track of which students come from a Christian home? (Remember, "under God" was specifically added to the pledge during the Red Scare as another way to distinguish "us" from "them.") Don't think for a moment that the Christian children (and teachers) aren't aware of the "outcasts" that blatantly deny God in the classroom.

Being forced to "choose sides" every morning simply requires kids to lie - giving into the peer pressure of the majority in order to protect themselves from teasing, ridicule, and prejudicial treatment. I have known very few grade schoolers that would be equipped to stand against the group mentality, nor should they ever be put in a position to do so. Instead, they are forced to give in to subtle indoctrination of being "under God" as they subconciously accept the cultural norm of American Christianity. *One Nation Under God, In God We Trust, God Bless America, God Bless Our Troops!*

Agree and conform or.... (Now might be a good time to remind you of studies that show a majority of Christians regarding atheists as "worse" than rapists: *http://tinyurl.com/mxqqp4r*)

A flip question might be: How would Christian

families feel if their kids were forced to say "under Vishnu" or "under Allah" at the end of the pledge? It's amazing how one word changes everything!

NOT TO MENTION: Are non-believing teachers really allowed to omit "under God" as they lead their classes in the pledge? Professionally or socially? Can you imagine the outrage from "real God-fearing American" (Christian) parents? I am convinced that in the vast majority of classrooms my kids have been in - this would have sparked a major-but-secret campaign against the teacher by concerned parents. So, some teachers have to lie, just like their students - all to avoid... *shame.*

IRONY: As far as "forcing their beliefs onto the world," I don't remember the last time an atheist knocked on my door, preached from street corners, had entire church outreach departments, set up TV and radio stations, or launched multi-million dollar organizations to send missionaries around the world to "force" their *lack* of beliefs on anyone...The irony of my friend's own remarks related to "forcing beliefs onto the world" gave me a little giggle. (This, coming from a man who used to be a leader of a large international evangelism ministry...)

Yes, I run a Facebook page that invites people to think critically about the Bible at their will. This, however, doesn't *force* anybody to do anything...

Remember folks, don't take your freedom for granted! Brave men and women left their homeland to avoid state-sponsored religious oppression and persecution for their own beliefs. Eventually colonies were formed, wars were waged, and a constitution was formed that promised the separation of church and state. Thus, the lawsuit.

I am proud to be an American who just happens to no longer believe that he lives "Under God." Please stop making me say otherwise.

www.AwkwardMomentsBible.com/UnderGod

The Latest Holy War

"We know we are locked in a war against the Christian faith, not culture." These are the words of Franklin Graham (son of mega-evangelist Billy Graham) from his February 2014 article *Ducking the Issue,* which I can only describe as a battle cry for modern mainstream Christians to rise up and fight a new holy war of their own.

Using that week's poster child of persecution for Biblically-backed intolerance as an example, Graham explains that the reason there was such backlash against the anti-gay and racially ignorant remarks made by Phil Robertson (of *Duck Dynasty*) was because *"he brought them face to face with their sinful state."* Graham continues, *"Christians and the Christian faith are under intense attack today,"* further claiming that the *"worldly systems of politics, courts, entertainment and education can be instruments of devilish harm unless they are under the influence of Christian precepts."*

It doesn't take Graham long before he ramps up the all-too-familiar rhetoric of fear and persecution to assert, *"the enemy of our souls is working his wicked schemes that seek to suppress and oppress believers,"* going as far as to add a dramatic flair about the *"rising tide of evil and iniquity that threatens to engulf our nation."* He then convicts his readers, challenging anyone who dares to call themselves Christians to stand up and fight against the *"full-scale assault against Christianity and the followers of Christ."* (Of course, all of this amid apocalyptic ramblings about Satan becoming more fierce and controlling the liberal agenda because he knows he'll be cast into a lake of fire soon, etc...)

Graham skillfully goes as far as to create a bizarre metaphor where homosexuals are apparently now the Nazis and if Christians don't stand against them, it will lead to their own demise. To finish this point, he presents a poem attributed to Martin Niemöller, a German church leader who eventually stood against Hitler, *"First they came for the Communists, but I was not a Communist so I did not speak out. Then they came for the Socialists and the Trade Unionists, but I was neither, so I did not speak out. Then they came for the Jews, but I was not a Jew so I did not speak out. And when they came for me, there was no one left to speak out for me."*

Wait! Two people in love, who have lived together for twenty years (in hiding, to avoid *actual* persecution) want to get married and suddenly Graham's fellow Christians are being marched to death camps? Talk about a persecution complex and dream of martyrdom!?!?

HE'S NOT WRONG: I fully understand why Graham firmly believes that he is standing up for Christ by standing against homosexuals - much like opponents of the Civil Rights movement or Women's Suffrage may have felt inspired to reaffirm oppression in the name of the Lord. In short, he has been taught that he's always right. After all, he is holding the manual to life right there in his hand. This isn't to say that Graham is distorting the Bible's teaching. He is absolutely preaching

according to *his* Word of God. But, isn't that just one of the problems with basing your life on a book that also supports slavery, rape, genocide, and abandoning your family to follow Christ? By now, it should be no surprise that Graham ends his inspirational draft speech by quoting 1 Cor 16:13 to his new recruits, *"Now is the time to be watchful, stand firm in the faith, act like men, be strong."*

FAIR WARNING TO CHRISTIANS: If you don't want to be seen as one of the same hate-filled bigots that speaks on behalf of all Christians - it is your responsibility to stand against those who speak hatred on behalf of your chosen religion. Just like the Christians who used the Bible to oppose equal civil rights for people of different color or withholding the right to vote from those of a different gender, the Grahams will also find themselves on the wrong side of history - bringing shame not just on their family name, but on Christianity as a whole. In 50 years (hopefully much sooner), it will be Graham that the church apologizes for. Silence is agreement. Speak up!

FINAL THOUGHT: You want a Holy War, Mr. Graham? I think you've got it!

www.AwkwardMomentsBible.com/HolyWar

The Ultimate Privilege?

I'll say it. Christianity has a martyr problem.

The point of this image is not to suggest that Christians are suicide bombers or to focus on violence from the Christian community (bombing abortion clinics, attacking gays, or starting wars with rival nations). It is about martyrdom. Sometimes we simply use "shocking" modern imagery to connect the dots of historical or cultural context.

The point is to open an important discussion about how some people are more than willing to die to prove their faith. The specifics of how the end result is accomplished seem irrelevant - dead is dead.

Of course, in our post-Crusades era, most Christian martyrs do not kill others in their 'ultimate sacrifice' - just themselves. They don't strap bombs to their chests, they just preach where they aren't welcome. They distribute Bibles illegally, then act surprised when they are arrested for breaking the law, and spend the rest of their lives in a foreign jail cell. They might infiltrate indigenous tribes, ending up cannibalized for knowing nothing of the culture or customs. Sad? Yes! But, does one man's indignant willingness to die for his beliefs make them any more true? Obviously, no.

We have all known martyrs. Some made the *ultimate sacrifice* in order to earn the *ultimate privilege* of a Christian by dying for their **beliefs**. Others may have simply disowned their family and friends to put their relationship with Jesus above all others. All felt truly convicted by Bible verses and their religious convictions. I have also known many widows, widowers, orphans, parents and children who have lived beyond the lives of these martyrs. Some show tears of great pride for the "honorable death" of their loved ones. Though, most show only tears of confusion, pain, and a helpless sorrow.

For those who object to the idea of Christianity having a martyr problem, I invite you to check out a few of these Christian classics that can be found on the shelves of most churches and Christian schools everywhere: *By Their Blood, Foxe's Book of Martyrs, Martyr's Grace, The Martyr's Mirror,* and *Suffering, Martyrdom, and Rewards in Heaven.*

There are dozens of titles celebrating martyrs, martyrdom, and the rewards you will get for paying the "ultimate price" for your faith. There is even a series of **actual children's books**, *Ten Girls Who Didn't Give In: Inspiring Stories of Martyrs* by Irene Howat. Yes, books glorifying martyrdom aimed at children - complete with motivational prayers at the end of each chapter. *I'm next, Lord!*

Don't even get me started on the relatively contemporary series of *Jesus Freaks* books from DC Talk - strategically aimed at teens. Martyr mania...

The only way I can describe all of these books is to label them as dangerous propaganda. They may as well have celebrity martyr trading cards to really get the youth excited about the privilege of martyrdom! This kind of rhetoric gets young Christians killed, shortly after getting all inspired and idealistic about preaching the Gospel in places where it's not welcome, begging the U.S. State Department to come bail them out. If everything goes wrong, at least they'll die a martyr, a new hero of Christianity, an example of true devotion. A new candidate for the Martyr Trading Cards!

I'll admit, I agonized over whether or not to release this illustration, as I knew it might offend some Christians. But why? Is martyrdom the ultimate privilege for a Christian, or not?

"God is great!" (You can say it in English all you want, but many would just as easily recognize this phrase as, "Allahu akbar!").

www.AwkwardMomentsBible.com/UltimatePrize

Seeds Must Die!

I recently watched a CNN special about the Jonestown Massacre where 909 devout religious followers of the Peoples Temple Full Gospel Church (along with 9 innocent bystanders) died as the result of ritualistic infanticide, suicide, and murder once leaders felt threatened that outside influences might infect their utopian paradise. Kool-Aid cliches aside, 3 year-olds don't commit suicide - they were murdered.

By the time Jim Jones died, he had turned into a raving drug-addled communist who thought he was God. But, that it not how things began - it never is. Just before he was labeled as an "insane cult leader," Jones was a respected charismatic preacher from San Francisco who was regularly sought out by top politicians to rally the vote. Just 18 months before the massacre at Jonestown, he was chosen to lead 600 anti-suicide activists on a march across the Golden Gate Bridge to demand that a suicide prevention barrier be erected. (Sad irony noted.)

Among the dead was Leo Ryan, the only US congressman to ever be killed in the line of duty - gunned down along with the NBC News crew that accompanied the visit to the compound out of concern for the safety of the followers.

Watching the final footage of the aftermath, I had completely forgotten the eerily dark reminder of this sign hanging over the dead bodies in the main chapel. The entire story seems so far fetched, yet - so familiar. A reminder and a warning...

"Those who do not remember the past are condemned to repeat it." - George Santayana

www.AwkwardMomentsBible.com/SeedsMustDie

Plausible Prophecies

"That's just a crazy prophecy from Revelation! No real Christians actually believe any of that!"
- Trevor M.

Oh, really? Tell that to the **multi-billion** dollar Christian book industry that is absolutely filled with books and movies about the "end times." The rapture, tribulation, the mark of the beast, the anti-christ, armageddon - you name it! (I was always hoping that these locusts would appear in the *Left Behind* series of movies featuring Kirk Cameron.)

WAIT! Since when don't Christians believe in prophecy? Without prophecy, Jesus himself would just be another eccentric preacher. Yes, much of the book of Revelation reads like an acid trip but so did Ezekiel and Isaiah. Prophecy, posturing? Says who?

www.AwkwardMomentsBible.com/AnyDayNow

No, What If *You're* Wrong?

Many Christians like to defend their choice of faith while challenging others' faithlessness using what is known as *Pascal's Wager*. Back in the 17th century, French philosopher Blaise Pascal concluded that because God is **not** self-evident, everyone has to make a wager - to believe or not. Everyone. If you believe in God and you're right - the riches of heaven are all yours for eternity. Ahh, but if you don't believe in God and are wrong - you are doomed to the torment of the eternal fires of hell!

Many of faith consider this philosophical question as being foolproof and unbeatable - often challenging non-believers, *"What if you're wrong? What have you got to lose by just believing?"*

First of all, I'd hope that any all-knowing God couldn't be so easily tricked into handing out eternal life to those who believe "just in case."

As far as *losing*, I'd ask - how many families have been completely dismantled and destroyed when faith has become more important than family, ostracizing those who simply don't share a belief in a god that is admittedly **not** self-evident?

There are few things more heartbreaking than an unattended funeral. Yet, I have seen a few as the direct result of abandoning, even actively rebuking family and friends in *this life* by betting it all on an eternal life with a complete stranger full of fabled mysterious promises. When the last breath is taken, who will be left in this life to say goodbye? What are you willing to lose in this life in hope of an eternal life? Yes, there is a wager. **Bet wisely, friends.**

www.AwkwardMomentsBible.com/BettingItAll

A Note From Horus...

It seems that we don't stop often enough to give thanks and credit where it is truly due these days. This project would have never been possible without the unwavering support, guidance, and incessant demands of our fans! The response from our first book was deeply gratifying but somewhat terrifying.

Over the last year, I have personally continued on my own path of questioning and a dwindling faith. This journey has led to some very dark moments with my own family and friends and even death threats from complete strangers. Over what? Illustrating Bible verses from a different perspective.

Contrary to my fears, leaving the church did not kill me. In fact, each morning I rise to find myself surrounded by a completely new community - connected by a hope for the future that is truly awe-inspiring, scratching an itch that an empty promise of eternal life could never satisfy. Friendship - no strings attached.

So, if I may be so presumptive as to offer my friendship in return, I simply wanted to say, from the bottom of my heart... thank you.

Your friend,
Horus Gilgamesh

The Trinity

http://www.AwkwardMomentsBible.com/Vol3

Coming 2015

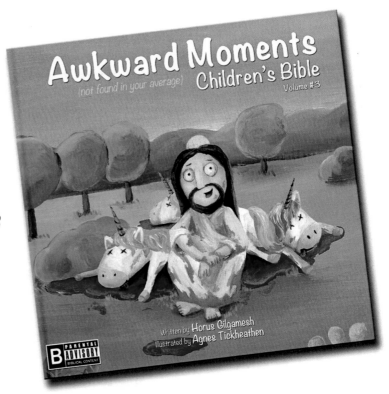

Awkward Moments
(not found in your average) Children's Bible
Volume #3

Written by Horus Gilgamesh
Illustrated by Agnes Tickheathen

B PARENTAL ADVISORY
BIBLICAL CONTENT

Made in United States
North Haven, CT
03 April 2023

34963580R00046